LET ME TELL YOU A STORY

LARADA HORNER-MILLER
HAROLD HORNER

Horner Publishing Company

To buy books in quantity for corporate use or incentives, call **(505) 323-7098** or

e-mail **larada@earthlink.net**

ISBN: 0996614419

ISBN-13: 978-0-9966144-1-2

❀ Created with Vellum

I dedicate this book to
HAROLD HORNER!

Happy 75th Birthday
And
Happy 66 years

On the ranch you love!

March 20, 1993

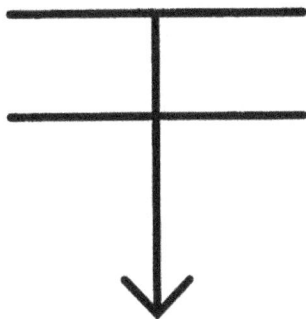

CONTENTS

ACKNOWLEDGMENTS

Let Me Tell You A Story is an appropriate title for the life of Harold Horner and the story of how the ranch he loves was put together. Anyone that knows Harold knows he is a master storyteller, so let me tell you his.

The source for this recount is Harold Horner, unless otherwise noted. To alter it much would lose his personality and ability to tell the tale.

Elva Horner assisted in getting the facts down on paper, by transcribing from a cassette recorder.

The last name for Scotty McClellan was debatable on how to spell and thanks to Jay Brown, the correct spelling was found.

INTRODUCTION

This story begins with Harold's parents and how the ranch came together. Then it continues with Harold's life and woven through his story is the continued story and influence of his father and mother until their deaths. The influence of these two people after their deaths also finds its way within this story, giving the ultimate ending. A sideline details his family life because this story of Harold Horner would not be complete if his family were left out.

GET FREE OFFER OF THIS TUMBLEWEED LANDED

Available
Now

Download free book!

Thank you for reading this book! Here's a chance to download & read another one.

Chapter One

HOW THE LAURENCE HORNERS GOT TOGETHER

Laurence B. Horner was born 17, April 1895 in Rocky
Comfort, Missouri to John Turner Horner and Matte Jesse.
He graduated from Horner Institute in 1912 and attended
Drury and Columbia Colleges for two years—one year he
attended with his father. He married his high school sweet-
heart, Larada Pearle Hinton, on 23 May, 1917 in Claremore,
Oklahoma. They both were living in Tulsa, Oklahoma. At the
time, it is not known which family moved to Tulsa first.
(Pearle was born 7, November 1895 in Beth Page, Missouri to
William Hinton and Minnie McDonald.)

The young couple of Laurence and Pearle rode a motorcycle to Claremore to get married with Pearle in the sidecar.
Laurence was 23; Pearle was 22. After their secretive marriage,
they went to their respective homes, not telling anyone, but
their families were not fooled.

Laurence and Pearle on their motorcycle

Laurence and Pearle's first child, Harold Laurence was born in Tulsa, Oklahoma 20, March 1918 on 18 N. Quincy Street. Their oldest daughter, Helen Pearle, was born 18, October 1919.

Laurence, Pearle and baby Harold

Laurence carried the mail in Tulsa. Harold got sick in 1925. It wasn't quite T. B.—a spot the size of a dime on his lung. He was taken out of school and under Dr. Deffenbaugh's special diet, the spot cleared up. But then asthma showed up. So Laurence traded jobs in the Postal Department with Mr. Bass in Branson, Colorado in April 1927. It was thought that the high dry climate would be better for Harold. He was taken to a T. B. Specialist, Dr. Shepherd, in Colorado Springs. The T. B. was diagnosed as retired at this point.

In Branson, the newly transplanted Horner's first lived in Dr. Blackerby's house (presently Jim Sheldon's house).

Blackerby House

Laurence and Pearle's third child, Joan Louise was born in Trinidad, Colorado on 27, May 1928.

In 1932 they bought the Readshaw house. This is the house they lived in and was the site of many memorable family gatherings until Laurence went to the hospital in July 1966. The house is now owned by Harold and Elva.

Readshaw House

The three Horner children: Harold, Helen and Joan

Chapter Two

HOW THE HORNER RANCH CAME TOGETHER

About 1928, Laurence bought his first cows and leased the Vinther Place. He was there until 1930. He went to Walt Cummin's Place (presently Vernon Sharp's home) for one year and then leased Dr. Blackerby's land in 1932.

Then he leased the Federal Land Bank land for a nickel per acre per year (the Bush-north half section, Arthur Rose—south half section, Ripey—Emery Gap, Rodgers——horse pasture and corral, Husted Place, Carter Place——south of road Hill pasture, Vinther—south of the road, two miles east). This land collection amounted to approximately 2500 acres all together.

In 1938 Laurence bought Federal Land Bank land, whose headquarters is the Rodgers' Place. Up until then, the headquarters had been at the Husted Place.

Helping Laurence, Albert Stevenson bought the Matt Posl land. Stevenson got a quitclaim deed from the Posl family in Oklahoma with a half a section costing less than one dollar an acre.

Laurence gave Stevenson one hundred dollars for his troubles and the Land still cost less than a dollar an acre. The exact cost per acre is unknown.

All through the depression, Laurence fought with a two thousand dollar debt (that doesn't sound like much today, but think of the times).

When he learned of the Doherty bid on the Federal Land Bank land, he talked to the president of the bank, Mr. Graham, about the fear of going deeper in debt.

Mr. Graham said to him, "If you are always gonna be afraid to do anything, you'll never get anything done," which prompted him to go ahead and borrow the money—about three thousand five hundred dollars—for the down payment for this Land Bank land.

Old Joe Doherty blocked Bernal country in New Mexico east of the Nigger Mesa. He came across the canyon and bought the Pete Nelson homestead. Laurence got the word that Doherty had a bid on the Federal Land Bank land that he had been leasing.

Doherty was trying to buy it out from underneath him, so this coupled with Graham's charge started Laurence to buying the land. Joe Doherty had a $2.00 bid on the land; Laurence bid $2.25 and bought it.

The wheeling and dealing done to put ranches together during this time was unique—one rancher would buy a piece of land in the middle of his neighbor, then vice versa. These parcels of land that divided up the unity of the ranches then became bargaining tools to get what they each wanted.

Anyone that's familiar with the Horner ranch knows names that identify certain areas: the Blackerby, Nigger Hole, Long Canyon, etc. But where did these unusual names come from—who were the predecessors to these familiar places? Let's look at the history and story that goes with each section individually.

Chapter Three

SIGNIFICANT NAMED PARTS OF THE RANCH

The Blackerby

Blackerby was a doctor. His wife was sick. Thinking she was going to die, he committed suicide. She lived another twenty years. When Laurence bought this part of the ranch, he paid Dr. Blackerby's widow ten dollars an acre.

Henry Brown and Lane Booher told Blackerby they'd top any bid Horner made. Blackerby's son, Bob, chose to sell the Blackerby place to Laurence for ten dollars an acre because Laurence had been leasing it.

Blackerby Reservoir

———

The Nigger Canyon and Long Canyon

In 1951, Laurence, Henry Brown, Jay Brown, and John J. Doherty got their heads together and traded around and made the ranches fit the country, particularly in Nigger canyon and Long canyon. Henry Brown traded two acres of rough country to Laurence for one acre of grassland. John Doherty withheld one lot along the Colorado/New Mexico state line that cornered with Mitchell's and cut off the east end of the land in the canyon.

John and Laurence agreed to a trade that was NEVER consummated UNTIL 1968, after Laurence's death. Harold and John finished the trade that Laurence and John had started. Horner's got the lot that joined Mitchell's; Doherty's got the east lot of Phillie land. John sold Horner's forty acres that had blocked the Husted canyon.

This trade put Horner land up close to seven thousand acres. The "Scotty" land was the result of the Doherty-Horner trade.

Mr. and Mrs. Sanchez had the oldest patent on land, dating back to 1880. This covered the Nigger waterhole and spring, as we know it now. This same couple had a homestead in Long canyon and died in 1917 in an epidemic.

Nigger Hole

Hogback Towards Long Canyon

―――

The Scotty

Scott McClellan dropped off a freight train in Branson and worked for Henry Brown (Jay Brown's uncle) from 1928-29. He lived in a one room house 8' x 8'. He then got logs off the top of the canyon, pulling them with horses. Doherty gave him the logs for his house hoping his generosity would result in his getting Scotty's land. Scotty dug the well by hand —forty-two feet. In 1980 Harold moved it to the present location.

Scotty made half the trail up the side of the canyon by hand which we now call Scotty Trail. He used a pick and shovel. The Horners finished it. Brother Jim came out from New York and built a two-room house for his folks visiting from Scotland.

Doherty bought the land for two dollars and fifty cents an acre. They farmed some.

Harold and Elva burned the logs from the old house as firewood but have saved in their living room an end log that has Scotty's name carved in the middle of it.

Joe Doherty bought the "Scotty"—lots along the state line —from Scotty McClellan. This was traded to the Horner's in the Doherty-Horner trade. The well was not operable when Laurence got it. He drilled it with a homemade drill in 1953.

Scotty Well

———

The Phillie Place

Charlie Garlutzo was working for the County Sheriff Department. Bob Gleason had "Phillie" (Philadelphio Cardenas) up on cow theft. Charlie got the one hundred and twenty acres bought from Phillie for seventeen dollars and fifty cents an acre while he was scared him about the charges. Garlutzo had the choice of selling the land to either Horner or Doherty. He chose to sell it to Horner.

Phillie was sentenced for a one-year term but got out in seven months for good behavior. Had Garlutzo not got the land bought from Phillie when he was scared, he would have been right back out there, back in business.

Phillie Place

Chapter Four

THE LAND THAT GOT AWAY

As in all land deals of the time, some of the land got away. Fred Hilgremand, John Bailey, Nona Wilson, Moffat, and Bar land was land all under lease. Henry Brown bought it all out from under Laurence.

———

As the ranch was going together, Laurence kept busy with his other job--carrying the mail. In a blizzard on November 7, 1930 Laurence carried the mail on his 64 mile mail route horseback. He rode one horse and packed mail on another horse. It took him three days to make the trip and he made the trip three times.

First night he spent with Roy Sheldon or Dad Cole; second night he spent at the Box Ranch; third day he came back to Branson. This very mail route saved Laurence's neck during the depression, providing a steady income and a living for his family.

Laurence horseback with pack horse

———

From 1934-1936, the First National Bank in Trinidad had only two cattle loans out—Laurence Horner had one and Bill Waldroup had the other. During this time, however, Laurence applied for a two hundred and fifty dollar loan for feed and was turned down. Mr. Jeffreys was authorized to give him one hundred dollars, which he did and told him to do the best he could.

———

In looking for water on the ranch twenty-two dry holes were found. Water was found at Emery Gap, Husted Place, and Harper Well.

Harper Mitchell dug the well we now call Harper well about 1951. Harold took the mill down the trail on a 1950 International pick-up.

———

Laurence retired in 1955 from the mail route at sixty years old after forty years of service.

Chapter Five

HAROLD'S FIRST CATTLE AND HIS LIFE

Roughly about 1929, Laurence bought Harold's first cattle. He took money from Harold's savings account, accumulated from doting aunts and uncles, and bought two yearling heifers for fifty dollars a piece.

Harold's First Cattle

During school, Laurence would trade Harold any heifer

calves for bull calves, trying to establish a herd. Everything in the world went wrong with the small bunch. Harold hoped to have thirty some-odd cattle by the time he graduated from high school, but instead there were twelve head.

In the fall of 1936, after graduating, Harold used these twelve head as a down payment for thirty-six head of cattle from Hank Webber for nine hundred dollars. This exchange started Harold's present day cattle business.

While Harold was still in school, he worked for Dick Louden and later during World War II. This proved to establish a life-long friendship between Harold and the Loudens, and Harold has many interesting and delightful stories and tales about his time on the Louden ranch.

From 1935-36, Harold worked in the hay at the Cross L Ranch under Cecil Shannon. Harold hurt his back working in the hay for one dollar a day. This injury has caused his back to still be a nuisance today.

In 1940, Harold and Mose Russell took over one hundred horses (broncs) for Tobe Brewer from Walt's Corner North of Branson to Cimarron, New Mexico via Trinchera, up San Isidro canyon, Bear canyon, down Yankee canyon into Raton, and south down the road to Cimarron. They cut the colts off in the stockyards and took the grown animals to Philmont Ranch.

In November of 1941, Harold married Nell Williams. Harold and Nell had three children: Fredrick Laurence born 17 September, 1943; Eva Larraine born 19 December, 1944; and Susan Liane born 12 April, 1946. In October, 1945, Nell left, taking Fred and Larraine.

The courts allowed Nell half of the cattle (107 head) and she hauled them away. This setback cost Harold about $7000 or $8000 plus 1/2 child support for three children. Child support went on until 1963.

Harold continued in his father's footsteps with an association with mail carrying—he was a substitute carrier from 1941-1972.

Harold bought his first steers in 1948. He ran sixty head on Horner land and made money. The following year, he bought Glen Watkins' steer calves, wintering them at Dick Louden's and brought them to the Horner's in the summer. They lost money. From 1950-51, leasing land from Excel Smith, the steers made money. He paid off debts and had $13,000 in his pocket. This was a new experience for Harold.

That fall, on August 28, 1951, Harold married Elva Dickerson.

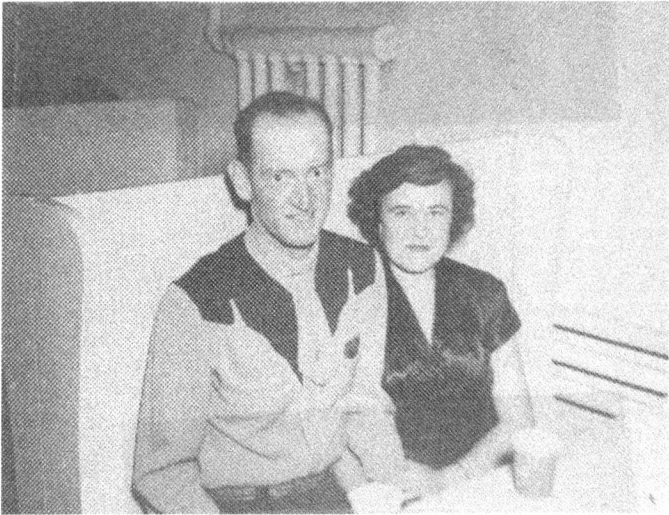

Harold and Elva

Chapter Six

SOME OF ELVA'S RECOLLECTIONS:

She remembers first seeing Harold on the dance floor and noticed his distinctive dance style. When he would walk across the dance floor, Elva would say to herself, "God, I hope he don't ask me to dance."

This happened at The Club Luna in Raton, New Mexico (now the Spur Club) and this is where it all started for them.

When Elva was twenty, she got thrown out of the Crystal Lounge in Raton; Harold who was thirty got thrown out, too. He waited a year until she was twenty-one to see her again after this event.

These newlyweds lived with Harold's parents from August until December and then bought the Stevenson house from Albert Stevenson for $3500. This price included everything—house, furniture and all. There was no bathroom or water or electricity. They put water in before the birth of their first child.

Stevenson House

Harold Virgil was born 25 May, 1952 in Trinidad, Colorado. As a child, Harold Virgil had rheumatic fever. Elva stayed in Trinidad about one month with him in a motel after he was released from the hospital.

The Horner' s house had four rooms, with the back bedroom running over with four bunk beds, two stacked on each other. Later when Sue was in high school, they put a two bedroom trailer in the back yard for extra bedrooms.

Teresa Larada was born 27 June, 1953 in Trinidad, Colorado, and the dancing Horners were square dancing the night before she was born.

Harold & Elva with their five children: Fred, Larraine, Sue, Harold Virgil and Larada

Today Harold and Elva have 9 grandchildren: Larraine's children are Jason, Travis, and Blake. Sue's are Jeff, Wade and Ellen, and Harold Virgil's are Connie, Andy, and Cheryl. On 21 February, 1993, Caitlyn Brooke arrived—their first great grandchild.

Harold & Elva with their nine grandchildren: Jason, Travis, Blake, Jeff, Wade, Ellen, Connie, Andy and Cheryl

Chapter Seven

STORIES ABOUT THE RANCH

This sideline tells the story of Harold's family life but back to the cattle and the ranch.

In the fall of 1951 Harold bought steers and put them on land leased from Excel Smith. In the spring, he added another one hundred head. That fall, he lost the $13,000 that he had made the previous year.

Harold and Elva struggled until 1954 and then bought seventy-five cows for $150 a head in Arlington, Colorado. He also bought one hundred thirty-five steers and went back to Excel Smith's with them, hoping the steers would help pay for the cows. But it didn't work that way—he barely got out on the steers and Harold hasn't bought a steer since. When he bought cattle after that, it was cows.

Harold got in on the Jean Oxandaburu estate and bought cows, giving seventy-five dollars a head. These cattle still lost money. That fall, he sold some for as little as forty dollars a head.

In 1957, Harold bought cows from Scott Commission Co. in Trinidad, Colorado and started making money.

Left to Right: Joan, Laurence, Pearle, Harold and Helen

In 1963, a horrible drought forced the Horners to sell out all the cattle. All that remained on the ranch was the horses. This was a sad day for the Horners. But Harold bought sixty-seven cows back in the spring of 1964. These cows were from Jim Patterson from Springfield, Colorado and were Anxiety IV cattle, a good line of Hereford cattle which has become the basis for what the Horners have today.

———

Horse accidents plagued the Horners in the early '60s. In 1963, doing routine cattle work, Laurence was bucked off of a horse by the "Phillie Place." Harold, Sue, Harold Virgil and Larada were all riding and witnessed this accident. He was badly hurt and this should have killed a man his age, but he was active and in good physical condition.

He landed on solid rim rock. He was hurt so badly, that he could not be moved; therefore, the ambulance had to pick him up in the rock pile he landed in. He was taken over Raton pass to Miner's Hospital and the attending doctor was Dr. Blakely. After his recuperation, Laurence rode again.

In October, 1964 a horse named "Mickey" bucked Harold off in the horse pasture. Harold Virgil was twelve years old, and he hustled back to Branson, driving the pickup to get Elva. Jerry and Lloyd Winford found Harold while Harold Virgil was getting help. Also, George Strasia happened by because they were going to brand that day.

Laurence stood on the front porch of their house that day, facing east, with binoculars—he had a feeling something was happening out on the ranch—and he saw Harold Virgil driving the pickup into town for help. Laurence drove Harold and Elva to Raton, New Mexico with Roy McMillan driving Pearle.

The attending doctor again was Doctor Blakely. He pinned Harold's hip. There's a 9/16 inch pin 3 inches long into the hip, about a foot long plate hooks onto the end of the pins and goes along side the leg and tied to the bone with four screws. The hardware is still there today.

Elva spent sixteen days and nights with Harold in the hospital. Harold wasn't allowed to step down on his leg for four months; therefore, he was on crutches for this total time.

After Harold was finally allowed to walk, he walked the circle in the Stevenson house. He would make twenty-five trips one way, then reverse, until he had walked the circle two hundred fifty times a day, trying to get his leg back to normal.

———

The last three years Laurence was alive, he had surgery four times—the horse wreck, prostate gland, repair rupture and neuro-surgery when an aneurism behind his left eye burst. This aneurism problem occurred in July, 1966. Laurence died because of this November 6, 1966.

That's when Harold took over the reins for Pearle, and she paid him two hundred dollars a month for running the cattle for her.

This ended a unique working relationship that laces itself throughout this whole story of Harold Horner—a father-son relationship that had been successful for its duration. They worked as a team and did it well.

————

Harold did other work besides ranch work in his life. In 1965, Harold worked on the road in the Toll Gate canyon all summer. He drove a truck around the crusher and operated a screen. In 1966, he again worked on the road job operating a "packer." These jobs were just supplemental; the job he loved was ranching.

————

1975 was hard on the Horner family with deaths: Helen, Harold's sister, died January 31; Eva Horner, Laurence's sister, died May 15; Ava Evans, Pearle's sister, died on Thanksgiving Day.

————

Although the times and losses were hard on the family, the cattle prices were good, allowing the handing down of money to the three children of Laurence and Pearle—$3000 each tax-free. This went on for seven years and when Reagan became President, he raised the limit to $10,000 per child per year. This continued for four more years, totaling $120,000. The grand total handed down to the Horner heirs during this time was $183,000.

––––––

For fifteen years, the Horners bought bulls from the Dohertys which improved the herd, but major changes came in the operations in 1977.

––––––

Up until this point, Harold had done no crossbreeding, favoring the Hereford breed. But in 1977, he bought his first Semintal and Hereford cross bulls from Jim Davis for the crossbreeding program which is still in operation today.

Simental Calf

His purpose for this change to crossbreeding was to increase cow and calf size, increase milk production of the cows, and produce bigger and better calves. The weaning weight on the calves was increased by 90 pounds by using cross-breeding.

———

Pearle Horner died July 9, 1985 in the Trinidad Nursing Home. She went into the home June, 1979 from her apartment at 601 East Main Street.

After Pearle's death, Harold continued running her cattle, along with his, and increasing the value of the estate. He did this until the estate was settled two years later.

Chapter Eight

IMPROVEMENTS ON THE RANCH AFTER HAROLD TOOK THE REINS

In 1970, Don Lewis and Jerry Winford helped John Clark clean out six reservoirs.

In 1975, John Clark enlarged the Blackerby reservoir, one on each side of the Nigger hole, the big reservoir in Husted canyon, the big reservoir at the Phillie Place, and Emery Gap.

In 1976, John Clark made three reservoirs in the canyon.

In 1980, a new barn, built by Peachy Green and Tony McDonald, replaced the old falling-down barn. This same year Ed Hollenbeck drilled three new holes and got water in all three holes. Bloyce Lampton witched all three holes.

In 1981, new tanks were put at two mills on the Bush Place.

In 1983, John Clark built a reservoir this side of the Harper well in the canyon.

In 1991 and 1992, the improvements continued concerning water on the ranch. In 1991, he replaced the wooden windmill with a steel tower at the corral—the wooden one had stood up for 51 years.

In 1992, two holes in the summer pasture ended up dry,

and a new steel windmill was put in at the Scotty Well. The old wooden windmill was replaced.

In the last five years Harold has centered the improvements on replacing and redoing the old corral, starting with the east side and new the loading chutes.

In the summer of 1992, he replaced the picket fence with wooden panels in the corral. In the water lot, he replaced barbed wire with steel panels. New gates throughout were replaced.

The original corrals were built in the early '40s. "Dad did most of it," Harold added, "using split ties."

HISTORIC CORRALS AT THE HEADQUARTERS

Corrals and barns, facing north

Corrals and barns, facing northwest

These pictures show the historic corrals and barns at the Horner headquarters.

Chapter Nine

HOW THE HORNER ESTATE WAS SETTLED

In 1988, the estate of Laurence and Pearle Horner was finally settled with much strain and heartbreak. Harold bought out Helen's children's one-third of the ranch, but try as he may, Joan refused to sell her one-third, which fractured and split the ranch Laurence and Harold had spent their lives putting together.

Obviously, this is not the way we wanted this story to end, but reality is—the ranch is divided!

And the truth of the matter is this: Harold followed in his father's footsteps making the ranch successful up to the present, during a time when many other ranchers have folded or failed. Harold has worked hard and can go East today and look at the land that overflows with memories of his father, his children and his grandchildren and can look to the future and all its possibilities, because the land is his!

Chapter Ten

GET FREE OFFER OF THIS TUMBLEWEED LANDED

Available
Now

Download free book!

Thank you for reading this book! Here's a chance to download & read another one.

ABOUT THE AUTHORS

Harold Horner was a cowboy first, a husband and father and then a master storyteller.

Larada Horner-Miller is a poet and essayist who lives with her husband in Tijeras, New Mexico—a town nestled in the east mountains above Albuquerque. She holds a bachelor's degree in English, with a minor in Spanish and a master of education degree in integrating technology into the classroom. For thirteen years, she was a beautician until transitioning into what would become a twenty-seven year career in education.

In addition to *When Will Papa Get Home*, her other publications include *? This Tumbleweed Landed*, *Branson-Trinchera Historic Photos* (coauthored with Tom Cummins), and *Building*

Capacity with the Common Core State Standards for ELA-Literacy (coauthored with Karen White).

For more information:
https://www.laradasbooks.com
larada@earthlink.net

f 🐦 📷

ALSO BY LARADA HORNER-MILLER

This Tumbleweed Landed

- Memoir
- 2016 New Mexico-Arizona Book Award Finalist - Biography (Other)

When Will Papa Get Home?

- Historical Fiction
- 2016 New Mexico-Arizona Book Award Finalist - Historical Fiction
- 2017 New Mexico-Arizona Book Award Finalist - Historical Fiction

A Time to Grow Up: A Daughter's Grief Memoirs

- Memoir
- 2017 New Mexico-Arizona Book Award Finalist - Biography (Other)
- 2017 New Mexico-Arizona Book Award Finalist - Ebook - Nonfiction
- 2018 New Mexico-Arizona Book Awards "Finalist" in 2 categories: Ebook Nonfiction and Ebook Cover
- 2018 Book Excellence Awards "Finalist" in the Memoir category

Just Another Square Dance Caller: Authorized Biography of Marshall Flippo

- 2021 Book Excellence Award Finalist
- 2021 eLit Silver Award
- 2021 New Mexico & Arizona Book Awards Finalist – 2 Categories: Biography Other & Nonfiction E-book

Coronavirus Reflections: Bitter or Better?

From Grannie's Kitchen Cookbook Series:

- *Pies, Cakes & Christmas Candy, Volume 1*
- *Beverages, Cookies, Meats, Vegetables, Mis. & Records of a Rancher;'s Wife, Volume 2*
- *Casseroles, Mexican Dishes, Relish, Sandwiches, Salads & Desserts, Volume 3*

FUTURE PROJECTS

- *I Said Yes* - how to write a biography
- *Eye Witness to Life*. To be released TBA. A women's fiction about two women who become friends over a strange event. Watch as their lives intertwine and heal.
- Three poetry books!
- And one more Tumbleweed book—more poems & stories about growing up in Branson, CO! There are so many!